# Making the B

# Your Guide to Thriving in New York City

**Making the Big Move to NYC** is your whimsical passport to the heart of the iconic city that pulses with dreams, drama, and endless energy. Through vibrant chapters, readers embark on a thrilling journey from envisioning their Big Apple aspirations to planting their feet firmly on its bustling streets. From savvy budgeting hacks, and navigating the maze of neighborhoods, to deciphering the secrets of real estate and soaking up the city's cultural beats, this guide playfully weaves practical advice with the magic that makes New York, well, New York. As the final page turns, readers are left not just with a roadmap to city living but a heartfelt embrace from the city itself, whispering the timeless promise: If you can make it here, you can make it anywhere!

## Table of Contents

Chapter 1: The Dream of the Big Apple

Chapter 2: Budgeting for the City Life

Chapter 3: Picking Your New York Neighborhood

Chapter 4: House Hunting and Securing a Place

Chapter 5: Making the Move

Chapter 6: Public Transportation and Getting Around

Chapter 7: Immerse Yourself: Culture, Entertainment, and Social Life

Chapter 8: Working in NYC: Navigating the Job Market

Chapter 9: Safety, Health, and Well-being in the Concrete Jungle

Chapter 10: From Tourist to Local: Truly Becoming a New Yorker

Epilogue: One Year Later - Stories from Recent Transplants.

# CHAPTER 1: THE DREAM OF THE BIG APPLE

## Welcome to NYC: A Symphony of Dreams, Delis, and Dazzling Heights!

Ahoy, dreamers and adventurers! If you're holding this guide, chances are you've been bitten by the "I want to live in New York City" bug, and you're on a mission to transform that scribble on your bucket list into a glossy photo on your Instagram. You're not just aiming for a pit stop; you're gearing up to call this city your home. Bravo!

Let's take a whimsical whirlwind tour through time and discover what makes this metropolis the stuff of legends. Hop on this metaphorical yellow cab; it's time to delve deep into the vibrant heart of NYC!

**From Humble Beginnings to City of Skyscrapers:** New York, originally named New Amsterdam by the Dutch settlers, was like that one quiet student in class who later became the star quarterback. Over centuries, from being a small trading post to surviving fires, riots, and economic booms and busts, NYC went on a dramatic teenage-like growth spurt. Now, she stands tall, adorned with skyscrapers, embodying the American spirit. And like any proud mother, the Statue of Liberty has been watching over her since 1886!

**A Melting Pot of Every Flavor:** Imagine stirring a pot filled with ingredients from all over the world. Add a pinch of Italy, a splash of China, a dollop of India, a zest of Greece…you get the picture. Voilà! Out comes a tantalizing dish named New York City. The Big Apple doesn't just offer you places; it offers worlds. Chinatown's dragon dances, Little Italy's pizzerias, the rhythmic beats from Harlem – it's a global gala here every day!

**The Celeb Connection:** Lights! Camera! New York! Marilyn Monroe once famously said, "A career is born in public - talent in privacy." Many celebs echoed this sentiment by making NYC their proving ground. From aspiring actors to renowned writers, the city has cradled them all. Ever heard of a chap named Bob Dylan? Yep, he kick-started his career in NYC's Greenwich Village. And if you walk the streets with an attentive ear, you might just stumble upon the next big thing performing at a hole-in-the-wall venue!

**Noteworthy Nods in Pop Culture:** "Start spreading the news…" and cue the rest of the iconic Sinatra hit. This city has not just been sung about; it's been celebrated in movies, TV shows, literature, and even on your coffee mugs! Whether you're 'F.R.I.E.N.D.S' obsessed or enamored by the magic of 'Breakfast at Tiffany's', NYC has a special corner in the heart of pop culture enthusiasts.

**Why Move to NYC?** Because Dreams! Ever had that one fantasy where you're donning your chicest outfit, holding a coffee, with the city backdrop, all while something uplifting plays in the background? NYC turns that reel into reality! But beyond the aesthetics, it's a place where ambitions soar, where every corner has potential, and where even the sky isn't the limit. If you've dreamt it, New York has a niche for it.

**An Ever-Evolving Adventure:** The best thing about this city? It never stagnates. While the classics remain – Central Park's charm, Broadway's razzle-dazzle, the Empire State Building's grandeur – the city always has something fresh to offer. New cafes, pop-up art installations, innovative theater acts, and mind-boggling escape rooms. Even if you decide to play tourist in your own city, every day will feel brand new!

Now, you might be wondering: with all its charm and grandeur, is NYC the right fit for *you*? If you're looking for a life that's static and predictable, perhaps not. But if you yearn for days filled with spontaneous jazz performances, midnight ramen runs, rooftop poetry slams, and an endless stream of opportunities, then you're in for a treat! There's a reason why they say, "In New York, the world's your oyster."

The Big Apple is not just a place; it's an emotion, an experience, and an adventure. If your heart's racing just thinking about it, you're already halfway smitten. Stay tuned, fellow adventurer, as the following chapters unfold the practical magic of turning this dream into your everyday reality. Let's hustle and bustle, NYC style!

# CHAPTER 2: BUDGETING FOR THE CITY LIFE

**The Great New York Treasure Hunt: Unearthing Gems and Saving Some Green!**

Ready to chase that New York dream without emptying your piggy bank? Fear not, for NYC might have a reputation for being pricey (I mean, where else do closets pass for studio apartments?), but with the right tools, tricks, and a sprinkle of fairy dust, you can strut around this city like a boss, without breaking the bank. Let's dive into this fantastic world of dollars and cents!

**Reality Check:** A Golden Glance at the Golden City: New York City is dazzling, but diamonds come at a price. Let's set the stage:

**Rent Roulette:** From penthouses that'd make Batman jealous to cozy basement studios, the range is wild. Average Manhattan rent? It hovers around $3,500/month, but trek to outer boroughs, and you might score deals below $2,000/month. And, if you're lucky, you might find a rent-controlled unicorn apartment where the price is as stuck in time as 80's fashion!

**The Takeout Tally:** $15 salads? Yep, they're a thing. But on the flip side, the city's also teeming with $1 pizza slices and tasty street food that won't munch away your moolah.

**The Commuter's Coin:** Those swanky heels are fab, but honey, the subway's going to be your best friend. At $2.90 per ride or $132 for a monthly unlimited pass, it's your golden ticket to the city.

**The Budgeting Ballroom Dance:** One, Two, Cha-Ching!: Setting a budget in NYC is like choreographing a dance. Some steps might be a tad tricky, but once you get the groove, you'll be twirling in no time.

**Rent Rumba:** A general rule of thumb? Don't let rent eat up more than 30% of your monthly take-home pay. For the math-allergic, there are plenty of online calculators that can do the number-crunching for you.

**Grocery Groove:** Farmer's markets in Brooklyn, local delis in Queens, and big-chain supermarkets can vary in price. Set a monthly grocery goal and stick to it. Maybe even treat it as a game show - *How Much Can I Save This Week?*

**Entertainment Elegance:** Museums, Broadway shows, concerts - the city's your playground. But remember to set aside a specific amount for fun and find ways to dance through the city on a dime – Free Fridays at MoMA, anyone?

**Money-Saving Magic Tricks:** Because Who Doesn't Like More Bang for Their Buck? Abra-ca-dabra! Watch us pull some savvy savings tips out of our hat.

**Roommate Revelry:** Sharing space can lead to shared costs and newfound friendships. Who knows? Your roommate might just become your partner-in-crime in this concrete jungle.

**Happy Hours and Food Specials:** NYC bars know how to treat you right. Look out for those glorious windows of discounted drinks and nibbles. Taco Tuesday in East Village? Wine-not!

**Thrift Shop Tango:** New York's second-hand scene is legendary. Grab designer threads at a fraction of the price and dance around town like the fashionista you are.

**The 'Extra Costs' Electric Slide:** Surprise!: Some costs in NYC pop up like unexpected confetti. They might startle you at first, but with preparation, you can catch 'em all.

**Laundry Limbo:** Many apartments come sans washers. Laundromats become sacred, and costs can add up. But look on the bright side: Laundry day can be social. And who knows, you might find your love story by the dryers!

**Broker's Ballet:** Securing that dream pad sometimes means dancing with a broker. Their fees can range from 12-15% of a year's rent. Pricey, yes, but sometimes it's the fastest route to your dream nook. For those that are reading this section twice, we were as shocked as you were to find that broker fees are a thing for renting apartments.

**Utilities Uptown Funk:** Not always included in the rent, and can vary seasonally. AC in summer can hike up costs. But can you really put a price on not melting during a NYC summer?

**Side Hustles and Money Musicals: Making Extra Dough:** The city thrives on hustle. If you're looking to add some padding to that wallet, the city offers a stage.

**Freelance Frolic:** From writing to graphic design, NYC is a hotbed for freelance opportunities. Sites like Upwork or Fiverr can be your backstage pass to the gig economy.

**Tutoring Twist:** Good at math? Languages? Dance? Offer your skills to eager learners and earn while you teach.

**Pet-Sitting Swing:** New Yorkers love their pets but are often on the go. Cue in the pet-sitting heroes! Apps like Rover can link you up with furry friends and some extra income.

**Financial Fairytales: The Legends are True:** You've heard the tales: The couple who found a rent-stabilized apartment overlooking Central Park, or the gal who scores free yoga classes in exchange for reception work. While they sound too good to be true, these NYC fairytales can be real if you keep your eyes peeled and your spirit adventurous.

Waltzing into NYC life without a financial plan is a bit like trying to salsa in flip-flops: doable but risky. With the right moves, however, you can make the city sway to your rhythm. Keep that ledger light, that spirit sprightly, and let the city serenade you. Ready for the next beat? In our upcoming chapter, we'll be diving into the eclectic world of New York neighborhoods. Get ready to foxtrot through the five boroughs!

# CHAPTER 3: PICKING YOUR NEW YORK NEIGHBORHOOD

**The Great Neighborhood Nom-Nom:** Biting into the Big Apple's Best Boroughs!

Grab your explorer's cap because we're embarking on a grand tour of New York City's neighborhoods. Think of NYC as the ultimate pizza, with each borough a mouth-watering slice, laden with distinct toppings. Whether you're hunting for the hippest spot or a cozy corner, this city's got a slice (or a borough) with your name on it!

**1. Manhattan: The Marvelous Main Course:** The heart, soul, and perhaps the crispy crust of our NYC pizza. Manhattan is where dreams, skyscrapers, and food delivery options (at 3 a.m.!) soar.

**Financial District (FiDi)**

*Benefits:* The pulse of world finance! Living here means being surrounded by iconic skyscrapers, the New York Stock Exchange, and the mesmerizing Charging Bull. The waterfront gives jaw-dropping views, while Stone Street offers an alfresco dining experience like no other.

*Perfect For:* Financial gurus, history buffs, and folks who want the city to mean business!

## Greenwich Village

*Benefits:* Bohemian roots, jazz joints, and tree-lined streets. Think cozy cafés, legendary music venues, and Washington Square Park. It's a mix of academia (thanks to NYU) and arts.

*Perfect For:* Artists, students, and anyone chasing those Bob Dylan dreams.

## SoHo (South of Houston Street)

*Benefits:* Cobblestone streets, world-class boutiques, and a vibrant arts scene. Plus, it's an architectural marvel with its cast-iron buildings.

*Perfect For:* Fashion-forward individuals, art lovers, and brunch aficionados.

## Harlem

*Benefits:* A soulful heart with rich history. Feast on cultural experiences from the Apollo Theater to soul food spots. It's also home to beautiful brownstones and gospel sounds.

*Perfect For:* Culture enthusiasts, foodies, and lovers of vibrant street life.

## Upper East Side (UES)

*Benefits:* Synonymous with sophistication. Here you'll find Museum Mile, upscale boutiques, and elegant eateries. Central Park is just a stone's throw away.

*Perfect For:* Museum-goers, luxury shoppers, and Central Park joggers.

## Upper West Side (UWS)

*Benefits:* It's the artsy counterpart to UES. Think Lincoln Center, Beacon Theatre, and rows of historic brownstones.

Plus, Central Park and Riverside Park are your backyards!

*Perfect For:* Art lovers, families, and anyone who loves a good bagel.

## Hell's Kitchen

*Benefits:* Close to Broadway theaters and bursting with culinary delights. This is THE place for world cuisines and off-Broadway shows.

*Perfect For:* Foodies, theater buffs, and night owls.

## Chelsea

*Benefits:* Contemporary art galleries galore and the High Line, a unique elevated park. It's modern, chic, and super LGBTQ+ friendly.

*Perfect For:* Art collectors, hipsters, and High Line strollers.

## East Village

*Benefits:* Once the punk-rock heart of Manhattan, it's now a blend of the old and new. Dive bars, indie shops, and the beautiful Tompkins Square Park make it special.

*Perfect For:* Night owls, music enthusiasts, and those looking for a vintage find.

## Lower East Side (LES)

*Benefits:* The LES now boasts a vibrant nightlife, eclectic bars, and indie boutiques. Orchard Street shopping, the Tenement Museum, and the plethora of street art echo its storied past while signaling its trendy future. Not to forget the culinary treats - from the oldest candy store in the city to the most innovative eateries!

*Perfect For:* History enthusiasts, night owls, food adventurers, and lovers of eclectic urban charm.

### Tribeca (Triangle Below Canal Street)

*Benefits:* Family-friendly and super stylish. Think movie stars, film festivals, and loft-style apartments.

*Perfect For:* Celeb-spotters, film buffs, and families looking for a chic vibe.

**2. Brooklyn: The Hipster Hot Sauce:** Oh, Brooklyn! This borough is more than just a backdrop to many iconic films—it's a thriving melting pot of cultures, cuisines, and charisma. Come along as we hop through its eclectic neighborhoods.

### Williamsburg

*Benefits:* Hipster central! Think artisanal coffee shops, vintage stores, and rooftops with Manhattan views. With its vibrant arts scene and the Smorgasburg food market, boredom is not an option.

*Perfect For:* Trendsetters, foodies, and those who thrive on indie vibes.

### DUMBO (Down Under the Manhattan Bridge Overpass)

*Benefits:* This area combines historic charm with modern chic. Enjoy jaw-dropping views of Manhattan, unique shops, and Brooklyn Bridge Park's greenery.

*Perfect For:* Urban explorers, photography enthusiasts, and riverfront sunset chasers.

### Park Slope

*Benefits:* Family-friendly with a bohemian twist. Brownstones, tree-lined streets, and the treasure that is Prospect Park. Plus, a myriad of local boutiques and eateries.

*Perfect For:* Families, nature lovers, and those seeking a community feel.

## Brooklyn Heights

*Benefits:* Historic and utterly charming. Cobblestone streets, the Promenade with its sweeping views, and close proximity to Manhattan make it a gem.

*Perfect For:* History buffs, romantics, and cityscape admirers.

## Bushwick

*Benefits:* A canvas of street art and the pulse of Brooklyn's underground scene. Warehouses turned art studios, dive bars, and multicultural eateries.

*Perfect For:* Artists, night owls, and those with an edgy spirit.

## Greenpoint

*Benefits:* A touch of old-world Poland meets modern-day NYC. Quaint eateries, vibrant nightlife, and McCarren Park nearby.

*Perfect For:* Food explorers, indie film lovers (thanks to Nitehawk Cinema), and park loungers.

## Bed-Stuy (Bedford-Stuyvesant)

*Benefits:* A neighborhood with deep roots and beautiful brownstones. Culturally rich, with cool cafes and community gardens.

*Perfect For:* Community builders, architectural enthusiasts, and those seeking an authentic Brooklyn experience.

## Crown Heights

*Benefits:* A tapestry of cultures! The Brooklyn Children's Museum, West Indian Carnival, and proximity to the

Brooklyn Botanic Garden.

*Perfect For:* Families, cultural enthusiasts, and botany lovers.

## Gowanus

*Benefits:* Industrial vibes meet a thriving arts scene. Unique venues, artists' lofts, and the allure of the (once notoriously polluted) Gowanus Canal.

*Perfect For:* Artisans, music lovers, and eco-warriors supporting the canal's comeback.

## Coney Island

*Benefits:* Seaside fun all year round! Iconic amusement parks, the boardwalk, and the annual Mermaid Parade.

*Perfect For:* Beach lovers, thrill-seekers, and those young at heart.


**3. Queens: The Global Gourmet:** The most diverse borough, where every block sings a different lullaby. Bring your appetite and your curiosity.

## Astoria

*Benefits:* Get your taste buds ready! Home to a melting pot of cultures, Astoria boasts some of the best Greek food in NYC, alongside Middle Eastern, Brazilian, and more. Plus, the Museum of the Moving Image is a must-visit.

*Perfect For:* Foodies, film lovers, and those seeking a vibrant community.

## Long Island City (LIC)

*Benefits:* Skyline views to die for! A stone's throw from Manhattan, LIC boasts waterfront parks, art hubs like MoMA

PS1, and modern high-rises.

*Perfect For:* Cityscape admirers, art enthusiasts, and Manhattan-bound commuters seeking a respite.

## Jackson Heights

*Benefits:* The world at your doorstep. Dive into an array of global cuisines and festivals, celebrating everything from Diwali to the Lunar New Year.

*Perfect For:* Culture enthusiasts, food explorers, and those seeking a global village vibe.

## Flushing

*Benefits:* A bustling Chinatown, the serene Flushing Meadows-Corona Park (remember the Unisphere?), and a gastronomic journey across East Asia.

*Perfect For:* Food adventurers, tennis fans (hello, US Open!), and park lovers.

## Forest Hills

*Benefits:* Suburban feel with city convenience. Charming Tudor-style homes, the picturesque Forest Hills Gardens, and a hopping music scene (thanks to Forest Hills Stadium).

*Perfect For:* Families, architecture aficionados, and concert-goers.

## Bayside

*Benefits:* A maritime retreat in the city. Enjoy waterfront views, breezy parks, and the historic Fort Totten.

*Perfect For:* Water lovers, history buffs, and those who enjoy a quieter urban corner.

## Ridgewood

*Benefits:* A harmonious blend of old-world charm and hipster flair. Historic districts meet trendy breweries and cafes.

*Perfect For:* Vintage lovers, craft beer enthusiasts, and folks looking for a touch of Brooklyn in Queens.

## Sunnyside

*Benefits:* A tight-knit community with a dash of art deco. Enjoy local eateries, sunlit parks, and the buzzing Sunnyside Farmers Market.

*Perfect For:* Families, urban gardeners, and lovers of classic architecture.

## Rego Park

*Benefits:* Shopping galore and green galore! Rego Center for retail therapy and ample parks for a breath of fresh air.

*Perfect For:* Shopaholics, families, and Sunday strollers.

## Jamaica

*Benefits:* A hub of transportation and rich history. Access to JFK Airport, the King Manor Museum, and a lively downtown.

*Perfect For:* Travelers, history enthusiasts, and those valuing convenience.

**4. Bronx: The Bold BBQ Base:** Rich in history, music, and oodles of greenery. The Bronx beats to its own drum, often with some salsa on the side.

## Riverdale

*Benefits:* Suburbia meets city! Majestic views of the Hudson, tree-lined streets, and tranquil parks. A hint of the countryside in the heart of a metropolis.

*Perfect For:* Families, nature enthusiasts, and those who love a quiet coffee spot with a view.

## Fordham

*Benefits:* College town energy courtesy of Fordham University, shopping galore on Fordham Road, and the New York Botanical Garden to feed your soul.

*Perfect For:* Students, shoppers, and flower fanatics.

## Belmont

*Benefits:* Also known as the Bronx's Little Italy. Authentic Italian eateries, markets, and the feast of San Gennaro. Mangia!

*Perfect For:* Foodies, romantics, and lovers of hearty Italian debates.

## South Bronx

*Benefits:* Art, music, and hip-hop's birthplace. Vibrant murals, historic buildings, and a music scene that's unrivaled.

*Perfect For:* Artists, hip-hop aficionados, and those with an edge.

## Morris Park

*Benefits:* A tight-knit community, diverse culinary scene (from Italian to Albanian), and the famous Bronx Columbus Day Parade.

*Perfect For:* Community seekers, food adventurers, and parade enthusiasts.

## Pelham Bay

*Benefits:* Boasts the city's largest park—Pelham Bay Park! A world of hiking, golfing, and beach lounging awaits.

*Perfect For:* Outdoorsy types, beach bums, and those seeking a respite from city hustle.

## Throgs Neck

*Benefits:* Waterfront views, breezy parks, and a small-town community feel.

*Perfect For:* Seaside lovers, families, and those yearning for a slower urban pace.

## Hunts Point

*Benefits:* An industrial heartbeat with a growing arts scene. Check out The Point CDC for community-based art initiatives and events.

*Perfect For:* Artists, community activists, and those cheering for urban renewal.

## Kingsbridge

*Benefits:* Historic armory, diverse shopping, and the Gaelic Park offering sports and events for the Irish community.

*Perfect For:* History buffs, sports fans, and those wanting a multicultural twist.

## Bronx Zoo Area

*Benefits:* Home to one of the largest metropolitan zoos in the world! Lions, giraffes, and yes, zebras. Plus, a stone's throw from the Botanical Garden.

*Perfect For:* Animal lovers, families, and anyone looking to roar (or just hear one).

**5. Staten Island: The Savory Secret Sauce:** Often overlooked but brimming with hidden gems. And hey, who can resist a free ferry ride with a side of the Statue of Liberty?

## St. George

*Benefits:* The gateway to Staten Island! Catch those sweeping Manhattan views from the ferry, and then explore the historic St. George Theatre or the Richmond County Bank Ballpark.

*Perfect For:* Commuters, baseball fans, and lovers of panoramic skyline vistas.

## Todt Hill

*Benefits:* Feeling on top of the world, literally! It's the highest natural point on the Eastern Seaboard. Enjoy the upscale vibes and stunning vistas.

*Perfect For:* Nature lovers, view seekers, and those who fancy a luxe touch.

## New Dorp

*Benefits:* A blend of the old and the new. Historic homes meet trendy cafes and shops. Plus, the scenic New Dorp Beach!

*Perfect For:* Beachcombers, history buffs, and café-hoppers.

## Tottenville

*Benefits:* A trip back in time. Relish its rich maritime heritage, preserved homes, and the Conference House Park's peaceful ambiance.

*Perfect For:* History enthusiasts, serenity seekers, and maritime mavens.

## Great Kills

*Benefits:* A coastal paradise! Dive into water sports at Great Kills Harbor or stroll in the sprawling Great Kills Park.

*Perfect For:* Water sport fans, picnic lovers, and those who love a touch of the sea.

## West Brighton

*Benefits:* A vibrant community feel. Explore Forest Avenue's bustling shopping scene or unwind in the serene Westerleigh Park.

*Perfect For:* Shoppers, community spirits, and park loungers.

## Rossville

*Benefits:* Dive deep into history at the Sandy Ground Historical Museum or enjoy the contemporary vibes of waterfront dining and shopping.

*Perfect For:* History lovers, foodies, and those who enjoy a waterfront ambiance.

## Port Richmond

*Benefits:* A melting pot of cultures! Relish a diverse food scene, historic architecture, and the lovely Veterans Park.

*Perfect For:* Culinary explorers, architecture admirers, and family day-out planners.

## Eltingville

*Benefits:* Suburban charm in the city. Lush greenery, family-friendly vibes, and a stone's throw from the lovely Blue Heron Park.

*Perfect For:* Families, bird watchers, and those looking for a suburban feel.

## Stapleton

*Benefits:* A fusion of the old and artsy! Historical structures, a rising art scene, and the inviting Bay Street for shopping and dining.

*Perfect For:* Art lovers, urban explorers, and those seeking a mix of history and creativity.

Staten Island is more than just a borough—it's an adventure waiting to be had, with a side of tranquility. Discover its neighborhoods, embrace its stories, and let Staten Island's unique charm captivate you!

**Your Must-Have Neighborhood Notes:** As you're jotting down your 'Dream Borough' wishlist, consider:

**Transportation:** The allure of a place is directly proportional to how easily you can escape it (only joking... partly). But seriously, transport links matter.

**Safety First Frolic:** While NYC is generally safe, checking neighborhood crime stats isn't paranoia; it's just being smart.

**Amenities and Atmosphere:** Farmers' markets? Nightlife? Schools? Pinpoint what you adore!

Ready to seal the deal on your New York dream? Whether you're a Manhattan maven, a Brooklyn bohemian, or a Staten Island superstar, the city's smorgasbord of neighborhoods ensures there's a perfect match for everyone. Get out there and take a big, flavorful bite of the Big Apple!

And once you've picked your neighborhood pizza slice, join us in the next chapter, where we dive deep into the world of NYC real estate. Think of it as setting up your perfect pizza base – essential and oh-so-satisfying!

# CHAPTER 4: HOUSE HUNTING AND SECURING A PLACE

Ready to start one of the greatest adventures in NYC? We're diving into the thrilling, occasionally nail-biting, always entertaining world of finding your dream apartment. Grab your magnifying glass and comfy shoes, and let's uncover some urban gems!

## The Lay of the Apartment Land

First things first, get familiar with New York's housing vocabulary. Do you know your studio from your alcove studio? What about a walk-up versus a brownstone? Here's a quick rundown:

**The Classic Brownstone:** Ever watched a rom-com set in NYC? Chances are, the protagonist lived in a charming brownstone with a picturesque stoop. Located mainly in historic neighborhoods like the West Village, Brooklyn, and Harlem, these townhouses promise both character and those ever-elusive NYC feels.

**High-rise Apartments:** For those who like their views served with a side of vertigo, skyscraper apartments in neighborhoods like Midtown or the Financial District are the way to go. Why wave to your neighbors when you can *literally* touch the clouds?

**The Walk-Up:** Ideal for anyone wanting to get their cardio in! These are the apartments you'll find scattered around neighborhoods like the East Village. Elevator? Who needs 'em when you have good ol' fashioned leg power?

**Lofts in Former Factories:** Spacious, airy, and industrial chic. Former warehouses and factories in neighborhoods like Tribeca or DUMBO have been transformed into sprawling lofts. They're like adult playgrounds for the artistically inclined.

**Prewar Apartments:** These gems come with a side dish of history. Mostly found in the Upper West Side or Upper East Side, they boast detailed moldings, high ceilings, and more charm than a basket full of puppies.

**The Micro Apartment:** When you're keen on living in the heart of the city but also okay with a living space the size of a shoebox. These little guys have made efficient use of every square inch. It's minimalism meets Tetris!

**The Basement Apartment:** Or as New Yorkers affectionately call them, "garden apartments". Sure, you might occasionally have a rat named Remy cooking up gourmet meals in the corner, but hey, you get some earthy vibes down there.

**Shared Spaces/Co-Living:** For those who believe in "the more, the merrier", co-living spaces have sprung up around the city. Less traditional, they combine private bedrooms with shared common areas. Plus, instant roomies!

Got all that? Stellar! Now let's dive deeper.

## The Fab Four of Apartment Hunting

**Location, Location, Location!**

Proximity to work, subway lines, and that 24/7 diner because, midnight munchies. Think about what you absolutely can't compromise on. Want to be a hop, skip, and a jump away from Central Park? Or perhaps nestled in a quiet street in the East Village? Pin those places!

## The Budget Balancing Act

Recall our budget banter from Chapter 2? It's showtime! Set a clear budget for rent and always ask what's included. If you find a place that includes utilities, do a little victory dance!

## Amenities and Atmosphere

Do you need a laundry in the building or a rooftop with a view? Maybe a pet-friendly policy for Mr. Whiskers? Jot down your non-negotiables.

## Safety and Surroundings

Safety first, always! Peek at local crime stats, talk to potential neighbors and trust your vibes. If something feels off or you feel unsafe walking around, maybe pass.

# Apartment Hunting: The Adventure Begins!

## Gather Your Sidekicks

*Brokers*: Yes, they're kinda like the Gatekeepers of NYC's real estate realm. Some apartments are "broker-exclusive", so these guys might be your ticket in. Just keep an eye on those fees.

*Roommates*: The "Friends" lifestyle doesn't just exist on TV. Splitting rent means more money for those Broadway shows or late-night pizza runs.

## Harness the Power of Technology

Websites and apps like StreetEasy, Zillow, and Facebook are

your go-to digital compasses. Set up alerts, because NYC apartments get snatched up faster than hot bagels on a Sunday morning.

### Sneaker Time – Pound that Pavement!

Sometimes the old-fashioned way works best. Walk around your desired 'hood and look for "For Rent" signs. Plus, it's a good excuse to grab a coffee (or two) along the way.

### Prepare Your Show-Stopping Audition (Application)

Landlords want to know if you can pay rent on time. Have references, bank statements, and maybe even a letter of employment ready. This isn't the time for stage fright!

### Tour Like a Pro

When you visit, take notes, photos, and ask questions. Check for sunlight, water pressure, and whether the "cozy" apartment is code for "you can touch both walls at once."

### Seal the Deal & Celebrate!

Found your dream spot? Act FAST! Return your application ASAP and once approved, READ that lease. Prepare the upfront cost, and get the first month's rent and security deposit check sorted. When all is done, cue the celebratory dance because you've just landed a home in the world's most exciting city!

## Hot Tips for the Treasure Hunt!

**The Lease Lowdown**: Read. Every. Word. And then read it again. Understand terms, lease length, policies on renewals, and any other legal mumbo jumbo.

**Hidden Costs**: Is the water bill included? What about gas or electricity? Some costs might be lurking in the shadows. Shine a light and get clarity!

**Visit at Various Hours**: That serene street at 10 AM might turn into party central by night. Pop by at different times to get a real feel.

## The Urban Tale of Triumph

Ah, the quest for the perfect NYC apartment! It's an urban legend, a rite of passage, and an adventure rolled into one. And guess what? YOU did it. Welcome to the next chapter of your NYC story, where every corner of your new space holds a promise of memories, laughter, and maybe the occasional lost sock. Here's to your new abode, may it be filled with joy, jazzy tunes, and an endless supply of those iconic New York bagels. Happy nesting!

# CHAPTER 5: MAKING THE MOVE

With the keys to your new NYC kingdom in hand, it's time to transition from a dazed newcomer to a seasoned settler. Follow these steps to (logistically) make the move!

### Utility Check

Set up utilities such as electricity, water, gas, and internet. Some apartments may include certain utilities in the rent, so clarify with your landlord.

### Get Insured

Consider renters insurance. It's not always mandatory, but it's a smart choice to protect your belongings. Friends of ours have been saved by this in the past when their "garden" apartment took on a huge rainstorm.

### Hire Movers or Recruit Friends

Decide if you're going pro or DIY. If hiring movers, book in advance and compare quotes. If you're moving to a building with an elevator, make sure to check out your building's elevator reservation requirements. If calling friends, promise them pizza – it's the NYC way!

### Secure a Moving Permit (if necessary)

Some areas might require a moving permit, especially if you're blocking a street or need a parking spot reserved for the moving truck.

## Pack Like a Pro

Start packing non-essentials early. Label boxes by room and consider a "first-night" box with essentials (toothbrush, pajamas, etc.).

## Update Your Address

Notify the USPS for mail forwarding. Also, inform banks, credit card companies, subscriptions, etc. about your swanky new address.

## Familiarize Yourself with Building Rules

Get familiar with where to throw away the trash, how the recycling works, and if there are any official "quiet" hours. Know these to avoid the dreaded side-eye from neighbors.

## Plan Your Move Day

Chart out the logistics of the day. Where will the moving truck park? Who's doing the heavy lifting? What time will you start? Having a plan reduces the chaos.

So, cheers to your next act in this grand urban drama, where the cityscape is the set, the pedestrians are the chorus, and every sunrise heralds a new scene. Curtain up! Spotlight on! Let's dance the New York groove.

# CHAPTER 6: PUBLIC TRANSPORTATION AND GETTING AROUND

## All Aboard the NYC Transit Tango!

Ready to dive into the labyrinth that is NYC's transit system? Whether you're a "get-up-and-go" subway surfer or more of a "call-my-chariot" taxi enthusiast, New York's got your back. Let's make your daily commute as fabulous as a Broadway opening number!

### Subway: The Underground Express

**Overview:** An expansive underground (and sometimes above ground) train system spanning all five boroughs.

### Benefits:

*Round-the-Clock Rides:* These metal worms never rest. Need a 2 AM ride after a late-night pizza craving? Done!
*City in a Swipe:* One ticket, infinite adventures. From the Bronx Zoo to Coney Island, all aboard!
*Pocket-Friendly:* Why spend on cabs when you can zip around without emptying your wallet?

### Buses: The City's Moving Lounges

**Overview:** An extensive bus system that complements the

subway, often covering areas less accessible by train.

**Benefits:**

*Scenic Routes:* Window shop, people-watch, and city gaze, all from your comfy seat.
*The "No-Train-No-Problem" Solution:* Where tracks don't tread, tires do!
*Stay in the Know:* Handy digital boards count down to your next ride. Fancy!

## Staten Island Ferry: Sail the City Skies

**Overview:** A ferry service connecting Manhattan to Staten Island.

**Benefits:**

*Free Ride:* Yes, it's free!
*Stunning Views:* Get iconic views of the Statue of Liberty, Ellis Island, and the Manhattan skyline.
*Frequency:* Operates 24/7, with more frequent service during rush hours.

## Citi Bike: NYC's Green Steeds

**Overview:** Bike-sharing system with stations scattered throughout Manhattan, Brooklyn, Queens, and the Bronx.

**Benefits:**

*On-the-Go Goodness:* Grab, ride, drop, repeat! All at your pace.
*Green Machines:* Save the planet, one pedal at a time.
*No More Traffic Tantrums:* Whizz past those car jams, wind in your hair.

## Commuter Rail (Metro-North & Long Island Rail Road): NYC's Majestic Chariots!

**Overview:** Train services that connect NYC to its northern suburbs and Long Island.

### Benefits:

*Speed*: Faster than the subway for long distances.
*Comfort*: Typically more spacious and less crowded than the subway.
*Reach Beyond NYC*: Play tourist for a day and explore areas outside the city, such as the Hudson Valley or the Hamptons.

## NYC Taxis & Rideshares: Your Yellow (or Green) Carriages

**Overview:** The iconic yellow cabs, green boro taxis, and app-based services like Uber and Lyft.

### Benefits:

*Right at Your Doorstep:* From A to B in private style.
*Accessible:* Most yellow cabs are wheelchair accessible.
*Whenever, Wherever:* No timetables, no worries!

## Pro Tips:

**Mix n' Match:** Subway to bus, bike to ferry. It's like NYC transit bingo!

**Tech-Savvy Transit:** Apps like Google Maps, Citymapper, or the MTA's toolkit turn you into a transit ninja in no time.

**Stay Updated:** NYC transit is full of surprises – from "mysterious" delays to "weekend construction fun." Check for updates to avoid unwanted adventures.

**Be Polite:** Offer your seat to those in need, avoid taking up more space than you need, and, for the love of bagels, don't block the doors!

**Walk!** Believe it or not, many New Yorkers live their best life without owning a car. Why? Parking is as elusive as a unicorn, and traffic can feel like a snail race. Plus, think of all the shoe shopping you can justify with the money you save!

And there you have it! NYC's transit system is vast, but with a little exploration, you'll soon navigate it like a true New Yorker! Next stop: Conquering the Concrete Jungle!

# CHAPTER 7: IMMERSE YOURSELF: CULTURE, ENTERTAINMENT, AND SOCIAL LIFE

## Welcome to the Jungle... of Jazzy Joints and Juicy Jamborees!

Okay, urban adventurer, you've mastered the art of the NYC commute (and if not, at least you've got some hilarious stories out of it). Now, it's time to treat your senses to the cultural carnival that only the Big Apple can serve up. Ready to sprinkle some magic dust over your New York nights? Let's unravel the scroll of NYC's most scintillating scenes!

Artistic Avenues: Strokes, Sculptures, and Sonic Waves

**Museums Galore**: When you think NYC, The MET, MoMA, and the Guggenheim are just the appetizers. Dive deep into history, modern art, and other dimensions in between. Don't forget those "pay-what-you-wish" nights—your chance to soak in culture without emptying your pockets.

**Jazz Bars**: Go vintage at smoky speakeasies where the air vibrates with melodies. Picture this: a dimly lit corner, smooth jazz notes from the likes of The Blue Note and Village Vanguard. A drink in hand, and nostalgia in the air!

**Street Art**: NYC's streets are its canvas. Wander through Bushwick or the East Village. Every graffiti tells a story, every splash of paint holds a dream. And yes, these walls are very Instagram-worthy. Snap away!

The Broadway Bonanza: More Drama than High School Diaries!

**Classic Shows**: Dive into tales of romance, mystery, and magic with The Phantom, Simba, and Elphaba. And while you're at it, marvel at the ornate and storied theater architecture. A show before the show!

**Off-Broadway and Beyond**: The city's dramatic heart doesn't beat just on Broadway. Off-Broadway beckons with hidden treasures. And a play in a pie shop? Only in the Big Apple!

**Lotteries and Rush Tickets**: A Broadway experience without the Broadway price? Score those last-minute deals and give your wallet a break. It'll thank you with a standing ovation!

Cuisines & Cocktails: A Gastronomic Globe-Trot

**Melting Pot Menus**: From mouth-watering pasta in Little Italy to the spicy kick of Koreatown's kimchi, NYC plates up the world. Why travel the globe when Manhattan's a culinary odyssey?

**Food Markets**: Hopping from stall to stall at places like Chelsea Market, you'll dance a samba of flavors. Indecision has never tasted so good!

**Rooftop Bars**: Elevate your cocktail game. Literally! Picture this: a sparkling cityscape, a refreshing drink, and the latest city gossip swirling around.

Groovy Grooves: Dance the Night (and Day) Away

**Clubs and Lounges**: From thumping EDM beats to sultry salsa rhythms, NYC offers a soundtrack for every soul. Slide on those dancing shoes!

**Live Music**: Uncover musical treasures, from indie voices echoing in Brooklyn to the resonant chords of grand orchestras at the iconic Carnegie Hall. An aural adventure awaits!

**Festivals**: Be it basking in the summer sun at Governors Ball, shaking it at Afropunk, or twinkling with lights at Diwali, NYC's festival scene never hits pause.

Parks, Picnics, and Play

**Central Park Wonders:** Beyond the boat rides and naps on Sheep's Meadow, find secret spots, hidden statues, and romantic bridges. Every visit reveals a new secret!

**Outdoor Movies:** Imagine this: a gentle breeze, the iconic skyline as a backdrop, and cinematic magic at places like Bryant Park. Popcorn? Essential.

**Sports:** From world-famous arenas to local parks, bring out your inner athlete or superfan. Whether it's the drama of a baseball game or the camaraderie of a dodgeball match, the game's always on!

Networking Ninjas: Make Friends & Memories

**Meetup Mania**: Whether you geek out over 90s cartoons or find peace in morning yoga, there's a group waiting to welcome you with open arms.

**Local Hangouts**: Dive deep into NYC's cozy nooks. Each bookstore, cafe, and brewery holds stories and potential friends. Get mingling!

**Classes**: Embrace the NYC hustle with a twist. Swing, pottery, or maybe a mixology class? Make memories, master skills, and meet kindred spirits.

Seasonal Splendors: The City's Calendar of Cool

**Winter**: Glide on the ice at Rockefeller, warm up with hot cocoa from festive markets, and let the city's shimmering lights wrap you in wonder.

**Spring**: Frolic among the cherry blossoms, parade with style on Fifth Ave, and let open-air jazz uplift you.

**Summer**: Sink your toes in Coney Island's sandy beaches, indulge in rooftop movie magic, and savor every open-air bite.

**Autumn**: Join the spooktacular Halloween parade, lose yourself in Central Park's autumnal embrace, and yes, pumpkin-spice up your life!

NYC's cultural concoction is as varied as its subway lines and just as electrifying. Every night here can be a serendipitous story, a new flavor, a memory framed against the backdrop of skyscraper silhouettes. So, put on those dancing shoes, grab that museum pass, and prepare to be dazzled.

Remember, the night is young, and so are you! Happy adventuring, cultural crusader!

# CHAPTER 8: WORKING IN NYC: NAVIGATING THE JOB MARKET

### Hustle, Bustle, and the Big Apple Bustle: Finding Your Career Groove in NYC!

The Big Apple isn't just about Broadway, bagels, and the Brooklyn Bridge. It's also a booming bastion of business, a mecca of modern jobs, and a haven for hungry hustlers like you. Ready to rock the world of NYC work? Let's deep-dive!

The Empire State of Industries: Choose Your Playground!

**Finance and Banking:** Wall Street isn't just about power suits and fast trades. It's where ambition meets opportunity! Dive deep into the world of numbers and make the stock market dance to your tune.

**Media and Entertainment:** Whether it's Broadway's spotlight, the buzz of top-tier newsrooms, or the glitz of film premieres, NYC is your stage to shine and tell your story.

**Fashion:** From the glitzy runways of Fashion Week to bustling design studios, NYC is the world's fashion capital. If you've got style and flair, this city's designer boutiques and top brands await your creativity!

**Tech and Startups:** Silicon Alley is NYC's answer to Silicon

Valley! With a burgeoning tech scene, the city welcomes innovators, app developers, and digital disruptors. Dream. Code. Launch!

**Healthcare:** With renowned hospitals and research institutions, NYC beckons medical professionals, researchers, and healthcare innovators. It's where care meets cutting-edge!

**Tourism and Hospitality:** Skyscrapers, landmarks, world-class hotels, and gourmet eateries! The city teems with tourists, and if you've got a flair for service, come make their stay legendary.

**Education and Research:** Prestigious universities like Columbia and NYU make NYC a global hub for education and research. Shape the minds of tomorrow and make groundbreaking discoveries today!

Landing the Gig: Wooing Employers like a First Date

**Research, Research, Research:** NYC is diverse! Understand the specific industry you're diving into. Familiarize yourself with the top companies, their culture, and what they're looking for in candidates.

**Network Like You've Never Before:** NYC thrives on connections. Attend industry events, seminars, workshops, and alumni gatherings. Platforms like Meetup or Eventbrite often list city-based events. Remember, it's not just what you know, but who you know!

**Tailor Your Resume:** Customize your resume for each application. Highlight experiences and skills that resonate with the job description. With countless applicants, make sure your resume stands out in that New York minute!

**Master the Art of Interviewing:** Practice common interview questions, especially behavioral ones. Be ready with stories that showcase your achievements and how you've handled challenges.

**Show Your NYC Savvy:** Understand the city's pace and vibe. If you're relocating, demonstrate your commitment to the move and explain why NYC is the place for you.

**Leverage Digital Platforms:** Use job search platforms like LinkedIn, Glassdoor, and Indeed. Make sure your LinkedIn profile is polished, with endorsements and recommendations to vouch for your skills.

**Stay Persistent:** The NYC job market is competitive, but don't get disheartened by rejections. Every 'no' brings you closer to that 'yes'!

**Expand Your Skill Set:** Consider taking courses or certifications that are in demand in your field. NYC boasts numerous institutions offering short courses to boost your expertise.

**Be Prepared for a Fast Pace:** NYC operates at lightning speed. Be prompt in your responses, and if you get a call for an interview, try to be flexible with your availability.

**Show Passion and Energy:** New Yorkers are known for their drive. Bring enthusiasm to your applications and interviews. Show them you're ready to thrive in the city's energetic environment!

The Concrete Cubicle: Adapting to NYC Work Vibes

**Morning Hustle:** That morning commute is a rite of passage. Master the subway system, and maybe grab a MetroCard for good measure. Pro-tip: always have a podcast or book handy – it turns "sardine can" moments into me-time!

**Coffee is Your New BFF:** Discover the local coffee shops – from hipster havens to cozy nooks. A New York Minute runs on caffeine. Soon, you'll have a go-to order that screams "I belong!"

**Dress the Part:** NYC has style! Whether your office is chic-casual or fashion-forward, take cues from your colleagues. Don't forget those comfy shoes for your commute; switch to those power heels once you're at the office.

**Stay Connected:** NYC operates at 100 mph! Stay updated with team chats, emails, and maybe even a good ol' Slack meme channel. You'll be in the loop and laughing in no time.

**After-Hours:** Discover the city's vibrant happy hour culture. Rooftop bars, quaint pubs, or trendy lounges? The city has it all. Mingle, unwind, and maybe even network a bit!

**Celebrate Diversity:** NYC is a melting pot. Embrace the diversity of your office – it's a mini globe in itself! Learn, share, and grow with your colleagues from all walks of life.

**Be Friendly, but Genuine:** A smile, a hello, or a helping hand goes a long way. Build genuine connections. Today's coffee buddy might be tomorrow's project partner!

**Embrace the Magic:** Every day might not be perfect, but there's magic in the NYC air. Embrace the ups, the downs, and everything in between. This city has a way of turning challenges into beautiful stories.

Dress to Impress: Decoding NYC Office Attire

**The Power Suit Saga:** Think "The Devil Wears Prada" but with a touch of you! While the traditional gray and navy are always in, NYC loves those who sprinkle their personality into those suits. Pinstripes? Check! Bold colors? Double-check!

**Casual Fridays or Everyday?:** Many NYC companies are embracing the chic-casual vibe. But remember, 'casual' doesn't mean 'last night's pajamas'. Think tailored jeans, sleek sneakers, and a crisp shirt or blouse. Casual, yet catwalk-ready!

**Accessories Make the (Wo)man**: From statement necklaces to snazzy ties, accessories are where you can really let your personality shine. And, oh, the bags! Totes, briefcases, backpacks—choose something that's as functional as it is stylish.

**Shoe Game Strong**: Comfort is key, especially when you're pounding the pavements of NYC. Keep a pair of classy heels or brogues at the office, and commute in those comfy flats or sneakers. Because, let's be real, nobody wants to play hopscotch with sidewalk grates in stilettos!

**Weather the Weather**: NYC's weather can be as unpredictable as subway schedules. Always have a stylish umbrella or raincoat at the ready. Winter? Those chic boots and elegant scarves are your best allies against the Big Apple chill.

**Dress Code ≠ Dull Code**: Always be mindful of the office dress code, but don't let it stifle your creativity. Find ways to weave in your unique style. After all, in NYC, individuality isn't just celebrated—it's the norm!

**When in Doubt, Overdress**: This is the city of Broadway premieres, fashion weeks, and red-carpet events. It's always better to be slightly overdressed than under. Plus, who doesn't love a little extra glitz?

**Cultural Mélange**: NYC is a global melting pot. Embrace cultural garments and styles— wear them with pride and flair, and you'll not only look good but also feel good!

Unwinding: Balancing Hustle with Hush

**Morning Mojo**: Kickstart your day with a NY-style power boost! Maybe it's a sunrise jog in Central Park, a hearty bagel and schmear, or a mindfulness meditation amidst the city's morning hum. When you begin with zest, the rest just flows.

**Efficiency is the New Black**: Streamline tasks, declutter that workspace, and use tech tools to your advantage. By working smarter (not necessarily longer), you'll carve out precious me-time.

**The Lunchtime Escape**: Swap out sad desk lunches for mini-adventures. Explore a new eatery, take a brisk walk, or indulge in a short reading session at a local café. A midday break is your secret weapon against afternoon slumps.

**Post-Work Play**: NYC is a playground after dark. Schedule regular post-work activities - be it a Broadway show, a visit to a quirky bar, or a dance class. Turn evenings into episodes of fun!

**Weekend Wonders**: The weekend is your canvas, so paint it vivid! From art galleries to food markets, jazz nights to picnics by the Hudson, fill your off-days with activities that rejuvenate your spirit.

**Staycation Sensations**: Who said vacations need airports? NYC is a treasure trove of experiences. Book a night at a swanky hotel, visit a spa, or explore a borough you've never been to. Rediscover your city with fresh eyes.

**Tech-Timeouts**: Sometimes, the best way to recharge is to unplug. Dedicate some no-screen time daily, be it a digital-free dinner or a book-before-bed routine.

**Socialize Smart**: Mix business with pleasure! Networking in NYC doesn't have to be stiff and formal. Attend fun industry events, workshops, or mixers. You'll be surprised how much business happens over cocktails and laughter.

**Find Your Zen Zone**: Create a tranquil space at home, even if it's just a cozy corner with scented candles, soft music, and your favorite book. Dive into this oasis whenever the city's frenzy feels overwhelming.

**Remember, YOU set the Rhythm**: NYC might dance to a rapid beat, but you're the DJ of your life. Adjust the tempo as needed. Some days might need more hustle; others, more hush.

Whether you're wheeling and dealing with big city brokers or penning poetic prose in a quiet coffee corner, NYC's job market offers something for everyone. Each skyscraper casts a shadow of opportunity, every subway station buzzes with potential stories, and every New Yorker—yes, including you—brings their unique spice to this enormous career melting pot.

# CHAPTER 9: SAFETY, HEALTH, AND WELL-BEING IN THE CONCRETE JUNGLE

The Glitz, The Glam, The Grime: Living the NYC Dream (Safely!)

NYC life is all about the sparkle of Times Square, the allure of hidden speakeasies, and of course, those legendary bagels. But like any major city, there's a practical side to consider. Let's chat about navigating the glittering maze of New York with both style and smarts!

Stayin' Alive in the City That Never Sleeps

**Streetwise & Stylish**: Strut with purpose and grace! While NYC streets are vibrant, being aware is key. Opt for crossbody bags that are both fashionable and secure. Remember: looking fabulous doesn't mean compromising safety!

**Heels, Hustle & Hydration**: While you tackle the city's pace in those stylish boots, never underestimate the power of H2O. Find a reusable water bottle that complements your style. New Yorkers know: a hydrated glow beats any highlighter!

**Subway Smarts**: Conquer subway etiquette like a pro! Stick to well-lit areas, especially during off-peak hours. Keep earbud volume at a level where you can hear announcements and surroundings. That playlist can be fire, but safety is hotter!

**Midnight Munchies**: Tempted by the allure of NYC's midnight eats? Dive in, but wisely. Bringing a friend not only adds safety but doubles the foodie fun—after all, two food critics are better than one!

**Park Play**: Central Park adventures await! If you fancy a jog or a quiet read, staying in populated areas ensures you enjoy nature without unwelcome surprises. Always let someone know if you're heading out for a solo park trip.

Pockets, Purses, and Pickpockets, Oh My!

**Zip it, Lock it, Keep it**: Love your designer bag? So does that sneaky subway swiper. Zip up and stay alert.

**Wallet Wisdom**: NYC is a great place to flaunt style, not cash. Keep only what you need. And remember, a decoy wallet filled with Nicolas Cage pics can be both fun and a deterrent!

Health, Hospitals, and Clinics in a Hurry

**Fit & Fab**: NYC boasts fitness spots galore! Explore new fitness trends – aerial yoga, anyone? Keeping active helps to counteract those delightful NYC deli calories and keeps the adrenaline pumping for city adventures.

**Feeling Peckish? Go Green!**: NYC's health-food scene is a treasure. Dive into vegan cafes, organic bistros, and juice bars that offer nutrient-packed delights. Think kale salads, quinoa bowls, and acai smoothies - tantalizing and Instagram-worthy!

**Doctor in the District**: Find a health professional in your neighborhood and schedule regular check-ups. NYC's changing seasons mean adapting to varying weather, so having a local GP can be a game-changer for those unexpected sniffles.

**Late-Night Maladies**: Know where the nearest 24/7 pharmacies and clinics are. You never know when you'll need an aspirin or a Band-Aid for those killer new heels.

**Mind Your Mind**: The city's hustle is thrilling but can be mentally taxing. Embrace calming activities: join meditation classes, pen down thoughts in cozy cafes, or attend wellness workshops. NYC is not just about the outer glow but inner zen too.

**Community Cues**: NYC thrives on community spirit. Join local groups, attend town hall meetings, or participate in neighborhood activities. Staying connected provides a wealth of safety tips, health hacks, and a chance to bond with fellow New Yorkers.

The grandeur of NYC isn't just in its landmarks but in the life you build amidst its avenues. With a sprinkle of caution, a dash of adventure, and a whole lot of heart, you can enjoy the highs, navigate the lows, and truly make this concrete jungle your home. Here's to living large, laughing lots, and loving every New York minute of it!

# CHAPTER 10: FROM TOURIST TO LOCAL: TRULY BECOMING A NEW YORKER

## Becoming Part of NYC's Tapestry – One Pretzel at a Time!

You've made it this far, and now the journey truly begins. Leaving your tourist badge behind, you're on the threshold of authentic New Yorker status. This chapter promises to sprinkle a bit of that native magic dust over you. Hold onto your MetroCard; it's going to be an electrifying ride!

Mastering the Lingo & Behavior of a True New Yorker

**The Lingo Lowdown**:

*The City* = Manhattan. Period.
*Upstate* = Literally anywhere in New York that isn't NYC (except Long Island)
*Bodega* = Your go-to corner store for everything from sandwiches to aspirin.
*Schmear* = The generous dollop of cream cheese on your bagel. Yes, it's an art.

**Subway 101**: It's not just a mode of transport; it's a lifestyle. Know the difference between 'Uptown' and 'Downtown' and never, *ever*, call it a metro. Bonus points: perfect the art of swiping your MetroCard seamlessly at the turnstile!

**NYC Timing**: Remember, a New York minute is approximately half a regular minute. Everything's on the go, but hey, that's the thrill! Hustle, but with flair.

**Walking Woos**: New Yorkers walk fast, with purpose, and mostly in straight lines. Sidewalks are like highways: stick to the right and overtake on the left. Oh, and remember - stopping abruptly is the NYC version of a party foul.

**Coffee Culture**: Here, coffee is less a drink, and more an accessory. Master ordering your 'regular coffee' (a drip coffee with milk and sugar). And don't be surprised if your order is ready before you've even finished saying it.

**Foodie Finesse**: Dive into the city's food cart culture. Grab a pretzel, a hot dog, or roasted nuts on the go. And for the love of New York, learn to fold your pizza slice correctly (in half, lengthwise) for that perfect bite.

**Park Prowess**: When someone says "the park," they mean Central Park. Know the hotspots, from the Bow Bridge to Strawberry Fields. It's not just a green space; it's the city's communal backyard.

**Honk Hints**: Car horns in NYC are like bird calls in nature – constant, varied, and signaling all sorts of messages. From 'Move it!' to 'Hey, neighbor!', get attuned to the soundtrack of the streets.

**Neighborly Nods**: While the city is vast, neighborhoods form tight-knit communities. Join in local block parties, street fairs, or trivia nights at the corner bar. Be present, be genuine, and watch bonds form.

**Thick Skin, Warm Heart**: New Yorkers may seem brusque, but beneath that swift exterior beats a warm, welcoming heart. They'll give you directions, recommend their favorite deli, and jump in to help when needed

Engaging in True NYC Pastimes

**Park Picnics with Pizzazz**: Central Park isn't just green space—it's a canvas for leisure. Grab a plaid blanket, gourmet sandwiches, and join the local talent show. From impromptu dance-offs to Shakespearean soliloquies, expect the unexpected!

**The Rooftop Romance**: New York's skyline becomes even more mesmerizing from its high-altitude havens. Toast the town at a swanky rooftop bar or simply gaze at the stars from an apartment terrace. Elevation elevates the experience!

**Bodega Brunches**: Breakfast from a bodega is legendary. From buttery croissants to the perfectly spiced breakfast burrito, these corner shops are culinary wonderlands for those in the know.

**Speakeasy Sneak-ins**: Behind inconspicuous doors lie NYC's hidden cocktail realms. Know the password, push the right bookshelf, and step into a world of vintage vibes and concoctions that spark conversations.

**Thrifting Thrills**: Vintage is vogue! Delve into the city's array of thrift shops and flea markets. From retro jackets to antique trinkets, each find narrates a tale of NYC's rich tapestry.

**Street Art Safaris**: Skip the mainstream museums occasionally and wander through Bushwick or Williamsburg. Walls whisper stories, and alleyways become art exhibits, celebrating graffiti gurus and mural maestros.

**Pop-up Parties**: From immersive theater experiences to surprise gigs in parks, NYC loves its pop-ups. Always be on the lookout (or ear-out?)—the next big thing might just be around your corner.

**Bike the Big Apple**: Rent a Citi Bike and meander through Manhattan, coast along the Hudson, or explore charming borough nooks. Pedal-powered sightseeing? Count us in!

**Neighborhood Nosh**: Every borough boasts a signature bite. Dive into Queens for sumptuous samosas, head to Harlem for soul food, or the Bronx for a bagel that's sheer bliss. An NYC stay is a gastronomic globe-trot.

**Stoop Stories**: Ever seen those charming staircases outside brownstones? They're called stoops, and they're social hubs. Share a coffee, a chat, or simply people-watch. NYC's drama unfolds right here.

Embracing the Quirks & Wrinkles of the Big Apple

**Bodega Cats**: These feline emperors reign over the aisles. From guarding the cereal section to purring approval at your late-night snack choices, they're an adorable oddity every New Yorker secretly adores.

**Subway Serenades**: The NYC subway isn't just transportation—it's an underground talent fest! From opera arias to breakdancing marvels, every ride becomes a free ticket to Broadway.

**Mystery Liquid Sidestep**: Ah, the art of deftly avoiding that unidentifiable puddle. It's a rite of passage! Embrace the challenge, and consider it your personal NYC obstacle course.

**Scaffolding Chic**: These metal mazes aren't just construction essentials; they're New York's bonus architecture. Perfect for sudden rain shelter or an impromptu rendezvous!

**Pizza Rat's Fans**: Remember our iconic Pizza Rat, hustling with a slice? Well, NYC wildlife (from ambitious squirrels to Broadway-loving pigeons) showcases the city's hustle spirit in the cutest, quirkiest ways.

**Apartment Tetris**: Space might be a premium, but creativity knows no bounds! Transforming a studio into a multi-functional palace becomes a fun, imaginative game. Vertical gardens? Lofted beds? Bring it on!

**Fashion Fusion**: NYC is where Polar Fleece meets Prada. Where sequins shine at brunch and sneakers strut at galas. It's not just fashion; it's expressive, eclectic poetry.

**Time-traveling Bars**: One moment you're in a 2023 cocktail lounge, the next you're whisked away to a Prohibition-era speakeasy. NYC's nightlife is a quirky cocktail of eras, flavors, and tales.

The transition from a tourist to a true New Yorker isn't just about knowing where to eat or how to commute. It's a heartfelt connection, a dance of experiences, challenges, joys, and discoveries. You're not just living in NYC; you're *becoming* NYC. So, here's to every pizza slice, every subway ride, and every "Hey, I'm walkin' here!" moment. **Welcome home!**

Made in the USA
Middletown, DE
02 June 2025

76429842R00031